LIFE THROUGH POETRY

THOUGHTS FROM A DIVIDED MIND

COREY W. GIBSON

JP
Jan-Carol
Publishing, Inc
"every story needs a book"

Life Through Poetry
Thoughts from a Divided Mind
Corey W. Gibson

Published October 2025
Little Creek Books
Imprint of Jan-Carol Publishing, Inc
All rights reserved
Book Design: Tara Sizemore
Copyright © 2025 by Corey W. Gibson

ISBN: 978-1-962561-97-6
Library of Congress Control Number: On file

You may contact the publisher:
Jan-Carol Publishing, Inc
PO Box 701
Johnson City, TN 37605
publisher@jancarolpublishing.com
www.jancarolpublishing.com

LIFE
THROUGH
POETRY

THOUGHTS FROM
A DIVIDED MIND

CONTENTS

Author's Note iv

Foreword v

The Outsider 1

The Puzzle 2

The Whisper 3

The Ascension 4

Digital Death 5

Embracing Change 6

Crusade 7

Expectations 8

Hear This 9

Lost Time 10

Beyond the Culmination 11

My Shelter 12

Wreckage 13

The Invisible Haze 14

A Trace of Poison 15

The Enemy She Attracts 16

Shattered 17

The Door 18

White Shadows 19

Remembering 20

Taken 21

The Mask of Laughter 22

Irreparable 23

Disappearing Quietly 24

Listen Carefully 25

Familiar Battles 26

An Old Account 27

Footprints 28

Promised Peace 29

Against the Darkness 30

The Clearing 31

Acknowledgments 32

About the Author 33

AUTHOR'S NOTE

Thank you for picking up this book. I would like to take a moment to express my heartfelt gratitude. Thank you for your time, your presence, and your love of poetry.

This collection is born from struggles, truth, and painful growth. Each poem is a step through my difficult journey. Some were written in darkness, others in the light of understanding and clarity. I am thankful for the journey that led me here, for the people who stood beside me when I couldn't stand on my own, and for the courage to keep writing. Thank you for reading, thank you for feeling, and thank you for being here.

FOREWORD

This book is a collection of emotions torn from the pages of a life lived on the edge of chaos, and my search for something greater.

Each poem is a step in my journey through addiction, mental illness, heartbreak, and moments of revelation. These words did not come to me in ease or comfort, but in struggle and confusion. Some pieces are cries for help. Some are quiet prayers whispered to a God I'm still learning to understand. I've battled schizophrenia, the ghosts of my past, and the weight of my memories.

In these pages, you'll feel the sting of insecurity, the beauty of hope, and the strange peace that sometimes visits when my mind goes quiet. This book isn't refined for perfection; it's offered in honesty for anyone who's ever been lost. Welcome to the journey.

THE OUTSIDER

I walk in rooms filled with
voices, and none of them
speak my name. They see me,
but only in shadows, my profile
blurred at the edge of their world.

I search for the border between
reality and the constant whispers,
but it seeps through my fingers
like melting snow.

Their words are clear, but my mind
fractures them into pieces I can't
hold. I see faces twist into unfamiliar
shapes, eyes too bright, smiles
half wide, and I wonder if they
know what it feels like to have
your own mind turn against you.

I carry the weight of thoughts
that don't belong, fears that tighten
like knots inside my gut. And when
I reach out there's nothing but air,
nobody waiting there.

In the crowd, I'm always alone,
an outsider in a world that can't
see the war raging just behind
my smile.

THE PUZZLE

In the quiet space between us,
your laughter spills like daylight,
not loud, but enough to warm
the parts of me that I forgot
were cold.

We talk in fragments,
and I wonder how we fit,
these jagged pieces,
into something that feels whole.

I don't ask where you've been;
the past is a shadow we both carry,
but when your eyes meet mine,
it feels like the weight lifts away,
if only for a moment.

You reach for my hand,
not to heal or fix,
but to share the silence.

And in the stillness,
I find the shape of something new —
unhurried, unfinished, but enough.

THE WHISPER

I stood in the wreckage of my own making,
a place where light was a stranger, where every
breath was borrowed, and every
heartbeat a question.

Days bled into nights, and I
forgot the shape of hope, the taste
of morning. My hands, once steady,
trembled with the weight of choices
made in darkness.

But there, in the silence, where
the world had left me behind, I
found something buried in the ruins,
a whisper, faint but steady. It
spoke not of forgiveness, but of choice.

To rise again, not as I was, but
as I could be. To gather the pieces,
sharp and broken, and hold them
in the light without shame.

And now, on solid ground, the
echoes of that darkness remain.
Not of chains, but as reminders
that I have walked through fire
and found, at last, the strength
to stay.

THE ASCENSION

The bottle is gone, not
shattered, not broken, just
set aside. Its whispers losing
strength, its pull softened
into silence.

I walk now, barefoot on ground
that I once feared would burn.
But it is cool.
Cooler than those nights I
spent drowning in escape.

There is a sun somewhere,
not blinding, but warm, and
it touches my skin with a
softness I once thought only
numbness could offer.

I do not rise as a victor, but as
one who has stopped fighting,
who put down the war within,
into the gentle arms of a life
I did not know was waiting for me.

And here now, in the quiet,
I find joy. Not loud, not bright,
but steady. A pulse beneath the scars,
a rhythm that sings of tomorrow.

DIGITAL DEATH

Thirty years ago, the world was
quieter, slower. We looked each
other in the eyes, shared the same
spaces, the air not so heavy with
invisible currents.

Now, everything moves faster than
thought. Information floods like
a tidal wave, and we're all trying
to stay afloat, chasing trends, a
digital blur of lives not lived.

People once gathered in rooms,
talked, laughed, even disagreed face
to face. Now, our voices travel
through devices, our words reduced
to characters, filtered emotions,
likes and shares replacing connection.

Technology bloomed like wildflowers,
and walls grew between nature and us,
between truth and what we want to
believe.

The world changes, we built it up
and tore it down, while the horizon
waits for what comes next, and what
we will leave behind, for what we
still might save.

EMBRACING CHANGE

Spring comes first, a whisper
of beginnings, green grass
piercing through the thawing
Earth. We are tender and
delicate, hopeful in our innocence,
not knowing yet what the
sun can give, what the rain
can take away.

Then summer arrives, in its fullness,
in its heat. We think this
season will last forever, the
way we feel the warmth on our
skin, the way the sky opens wide.

Autumn creeps in quietly. Like
the falling leaves, turning gold
and red before they let go.
We learn to release, to shed the
weight of what we cannot keep.
The air turns crisp, and the wind
carries away things we have forgotten
to remember.

Winter comes, and teaches us to sit
with silence, to gather our strength,
and in the quiet something deep
within us is preparing to begin again.

CRUSADE

Through winding paths and
silent night,
we search for peace, an end
to plight.

With hearts weighed down,
yet spirits high,
we journey neath a boundless
sky.

Each step a whisper, soft and
kind,
in hopes to leave despair
behind.

Through valleys deep and
mountains tall,
we rise again to every fall.

In every tear, a sign of hope,
in every struggle, strength
to cope.

So seek we must, with courage, grace,
to find within a peaceful place.

Where suffering ends, and hearts
are free,
in love and light, eternally.

EXPECTATIONS

The weight is heavy,
not the kind that bends
your back,
but the kind that sits
behind your eyes,
pushing down every breath
waiting to see the look on
someone else's face when
they decide you aren't enough.

There is a silence that
comes when someone expects,
and it echoes louder than
any words, repeating the
question — "Will I let them down?"

So I hold my breath,
and I move carefully,
like I'm walking on glass,
like everything depends on me,
and I don't know how to
say that it shouldn't.

So I carry all those hopes,
and I know that there is
no chance for peace.

HEAR THIS

There's a world outside
where people move like shadows,
flickering in and out,
but the voices blur,
like radio stations caught
between signals.

In my head, there's a storm
no one can hear.
Words clash, images twist,
and sometimes the silence
is louder than the noise.

They say it's not real,
but it feels real enough
when you're the only one trapped
in the in-between.

I'm here and I'm not.
And the hardest part is
wondering if I'll ever find
my way back
to where everyone else
seems to live.

LOST TIME

There is a place
between breath and silence,
where time stretches thin.
An echo of all I've lost.

I sit there,
in that heavy space,
where light doesn't dare enter,
and nothing grows.

The air is thick with memory,
and I choke on it,
the past clinging to my throat,
like dust in an abandoned room.

There is no relief
in the turning of days,
only the reminder
that nothing changes,
but everything has already changed.

I carry the weight of nothing
as if it were everything.
It pulls me under,
deeper,
into the space where I disappear
and the world forgets
that I ever belonged.

BEYOND THE CULMINATION

I stand at the edge of
my old story, the pages worn,
corners bent with all I've carried.

The ink of my past still clings
to my skin, familiar and heavy,
like an old coat I've outgrown.

Today, I will close the book,
not with anger, nor regret,
but with a quiet acceptance
that those chapters must be
left behind.

Ahead is a blank canvas, a
space untouched by what
used to be. I inhale deep,
the air of possibilities, unsure,
but unafraid.

The burden lifts, and I step
forward, carving new lines
with every choice, and each
one a proof of my new freedom.

This is where I begin again,
not forgetting the past, but
no longer bound by it.

MY SHELTER

There is a place within
where the noise can't reach,
where the chaos calms
my trembling hands.

It waits, not with loud demands,
but with a quiet patience of
a tree rooted deep in the earth.
This joy is not the kind that
dances, laughs, or celebrates.

It doesn't rise and fall like
the sea chasing the moon.
It simply is
a steady unwavering pulse
behind the heart.

You will not find it searching the world
or seeking someone else's light.
It is the acceptance of all that is
and all that will never be.

Look inward, not to change,
but to see what has always
been there —
that which can't be shaken,
no matter the storms that come.

WRECKAGE

A heart once warm
now pulses slow,
its beat distant,
like footsteps fading in fog.

What once sparked,
now flickers faint,
barely a whisper
of what it used to be.

Hands reach out —
but the touch feels numb,
fingers glide through
as if the air itself resists.

The fire that burned
is buried under layers,
ice freezing over
each ember, each scar.

It is not hatred,
not anger,
just a quiet void
where love once bloomed,
leaving only the echo
of something gone cold.

THE INVISIBLE HAZE

In the depths of my mind, shadows
dance, and whispers of forgotten voices
weave a trance. A fractured mirror,
shattered glass, reality splits, a
ghostly mass.

They speak to me from unseen lands,
fingers grasp in my shaky hands. I
walk the line, a razor's edge, between
the sane and madness' pledge.

Eyes that watch from every wall,
silent sentinels that never fall. Their
murmurs seep into my veins, the
symphony seems like endless pain.

Faces blur and twist, surreal, nothing
is what it seems to feel. My world,
a canvas, torn and frayed, in frames
of terror, darkly swayed.

In this storm, I seek the light,
a beacon in the endless night. But
echoes of my past resound, in
schizophrenic chains I'm bound.

A TRACE OF POISON

In the quiet of a simmering
storm,
a fire kindled in my chest, anger,
raw and unrestrained,
bursts forth from its nest.

Words, sharp jagged glass,
cut through the air unchecked,
leaving wounds, unseen yet deep,
a trail of bitter disrespect.

In that moment, I was
consumed
by a rage I could not quell,
blind to the hearts I wounded,
deaf to the silence where
love should dwell.

Now, in the cool of reflection,
the flames have lost their sway,
regret, a shadow in the ashes,
lingers in the dawning day.

THE ENEMY SHE ATTRACTS

In darkness cast by moonlit
nights, my heart aches silently,
as jealous whispers start. When
other men approach with eyes so
bold, my love, it seems, begins to
lose its hold.

Their words, like silver threads around
her weave, a tangled web of doubts
that make me grieve. I watch with
silent torment, deep and stark,
as she does not push them away,
my heart left dark.

Each smile she shares, a knife in my
chest, their laughter rings, a silence
manifest. Her kindness, once warm,
now brings me pain, a storm of
fears that courses through my veins.

For though her love is strong,
true, and pure, this jealousy, a
wound I must endure. Yet still I
hope for more, and trust to light
our way, and banish the shadows
born, of my heart's dismay.

SHATTERED

I sit in the quiet, where your
voice once filled the air. The
silence is now louder than anything
I've ever heard.

I trace the outlines of your memory
with hands that tremble. Once
steady, now fragile, like the glass
I became when you walked away.

I can still feel your warmth in
the spaces we used to share, but
it's fading, slipping through like
sand I can't hold onto.

The world moves around me,
unaffected by the burning in my
chest. People pass, unaware of
the hollow ache that stretches
with every breath.

I'm a puzzle of what was, each
piece sharp, each edge cutting,
and nothing fits back the way it
once did.
This is how it feels to be broke
and left behind.

THE DOOR

I walk a path unseen,
through shadow and light,
seeking what lies beyond
the edge of knowing.

My questions rise like plumes
of smoke — who am I under
the chaos, under the weight
of a thousand thoughts?

In silence, I listen to the
whispers of something vast
and unknown, where my ego
dissolves like a ripple fading
on still water.

I step into the unknown,
not with certainty, but
with a quiet trust — that
the journey itself is my answer.

And as I explore the corners
of my consciousness,
I find not the end,
but the opening, the door
into forever.

WHITE SHADOWS

Tiny white circles, smooth
edges pressed into palms, promises
disguised as relief.
A swallow, a slide down the
throat, and the world softens.

The heart forgets to ache for
a while, but the body remembers.
It always remembers.
Soon, the hand shakes not
from fear, but from absence.

The mind no longer seeks escape;
it begs for balance, for normalcy
hidden inside bottles with
childproof caps that can't keep
out the craving.

The world sharpens again, every
sound scrapes the skin, every
light burns the eyes — and sleep?
Sleep is a battlefield where
nightmares bloom in chemical soil.

What once felt like freedom
becomes a cage, each pill a
rusted key that never fits
the lock.
And still, the hand reaches.

REMEMBERING

It starts with the silence,
a whisper that claws at the
mind, a need that's buried,
but never forgotten, lurking
just behind the eyes.

The days are slow battles, fought
in shadows and light, where
memories taunt like the bottle,
glimmering, just out of sight.

Hands shake with the weight of
the past, nights stretch out too
long, and in the darkness, a voice
calls back, soft as a heavenly song.

And the cost is written in scars,
etched deep in the soul, a reminder
that the fall is far, and the climb
back is slow.

For every day sober is a victory,
a step toward reclaiming the
light, though the road is long
and lonely, you keep walking,
fighting the night.

TAKEN

I found you, my love,
beneath the sky's embrace,
a whisper in the wind, a gentle
glowing trace. Your eyes, like
stars, lit up my darkest night,
and turned my world from
shadow into light.

With every step, you breathed
new life in me, a song of
hope, a dance so wild and free.
Your laughter filled the spaces
once so bare, and now my heart
knows love beyond compare.

In your arms, I found where
I belong, a melody that's true,
a never-ending song. Each beat,
a joy that words cannot convey,
a love that grows with every
passing day.

No more searching, for now
I clearly see, the gift of you
was always meant for me.
My heart, once heavy, now
is light and whole, overflowing
with the joy you bring my soul.

THE MASK OF LAUGHTER

A joke lands in the middle
of the room, sharp as glass,
but everyone laughs, as if it
didn't cut.

Sarcasm drips from tongues
like honey gone sour, sweet
enough to remind us that truth
hides in the corners.

The punchlines act as
shields, each chuckle a
small deflection from the
questions no one wants
to ask.

Humor…the bring light
in a dim rom, blinding
enough to forget what
shadows feel like.

But when the laughter
fades, the silence knows
better.

IRREPARABLE

The mirror cracked one morning,
but I kept looking anyway,
as if the broken pieces could still
show me something whole.

I walk through days like a stranger
in my own skin, touching walls
that don't remember my hands.
Memories scattered across the floor,
sharp edges of what used to be.

I step around them carefully,
but sometimes, the smallest piece
finds its way beneath my skin.
There's no map for this kind of
ruin, no guide for the hollow
spaces where laughter used to live.

I breathe in, and out,
as if that alone can stitch the
cracks together. But some things
don't mend. Some things remain
exactly as they are.

DISAPPEARING QUIETLY

His room is a dim, unmoving
place. The walls sag under
the weight of silence.
Morning leaks through the
blinds, but he doesn't lift
his head to see it.

The bed holds him like
an anchor. Each breath feels
borrowed, each moment stretches
thin, a thread fraying at both ends.

Outside the world hums, cars
slide past, people laugh in
fragments that can't be held
onto. It all feels like a story
he was never written into.

Food grows cold on the table,
calls go unanswered, and the
mirror reflects a stranger with
hollow eyes and a face he doesn't
claim.

Time doesn't move here; it
folds in on itself, and he wonders
if disappearing would feel any
different than this.

LISTEN CAREFULLY

A young man stands at the
edge of the world,
not a cliff, not a hill,
but a room where silence
should sit,
except it's never quiet.

The voices whisper,
soft at first, like wind
through the trees,
then louder, crashing like waves,
drowning the thoughts he wants
to hear.

His friends don't see it.
They only see him staring
off, like he's somewhere else.
He wishes for just one moment,
stillness, where his head is his own
and the world stops spinning.

But for now, he stands
at the edge,
waiting for the storm
to pass.

FAMILIAR BATTLES

A darkness creeps where
light once brightly shone.
Its whispers call with
promises untrue.

I face this fight but often
feel alone,
a battle fought with
demons old and new —
each step heavy with regret,
a chain that pulls me deeper
into night.

Though hope still flickers,
I can't find it yet.
It hides behind the lies
I've learned to fight.

But somewhere in this
storm, a voice remains,
a distant echo, soft yet
full of might.

It tells me I can break
these heavy chains
and find my way back
to the warmth of light.

AN OLD ACCOUNT

My heart once happy, now it
feels so sad.
You said you cared, but left
me all alone.
I trusted you, and now it
hurts so bad.
It's like I lost a part that was
my own.

I thought we'd laugh and
always be best friends,
but now you walk away
without a glance.
I guess some things don't
have the happy ends,
and I won't get another
second chance.

I wonder what I did to
make you leave,
or if you just got bored and
didn't care.
Now all that's left is for me
to grieve,
and hope one day that life
will be more fair.

But even though my heart is full of pain,
the rain soon will come after.

FOOTPRINTS

The path is worn, yet
unfamiliar, stone edges
softened by time and absence.
I do not step so much as
drift, a breath returning
to the lungs of the past.

The gate stands where it
always stood, iron and wood,
rust and memory, unchanged,
yet everything behind it
has reshaped itself in my
absence.

I raise my hand, fingertips
grazing the latch, cold,
unmoved by the weight of
years gone by. The wind
carries whispers of voices
I once knew — some still waiting,
some long gone.

Stepping through, I expect the
earth to know me, to sigh
with recognition, to fold me
into itself. But I am a
stranger here now, walking in
footprints that no longer fit.

PROMISED PEACE

There is a quiet joy in
waking early, the world
still stretching, yawning
into the day. A cup of coffee,
a breath of cold air, the
certainty that you are exactly
where you should be.

Success is not the roar of
applause but the steady
hum of a life well built —
bills paid on time, promises
kept, knowing your word is
as firm as stone.

It is the peace in your own
company, the weight of
responsibility sitting comfortably
on shoulders grown strong
enough to bear it.

There was a time when chaos
called louder, when the easy
road seemed the only road,
but now the struggle is different.

There is nothing to escape from
anymore. Only the beauty of
a balanced life. The pride of
standing tall inside your own story.

AGAINST THE DARKNESS

I spent years tangled in
shadows, where smoke and
bottles blurred the days, a
life built on unstable foundations,
nights I can't remember, wounds
I can't forget.

There were moments, fleeting,
like whispers. A flicker of
who I could have been. Those
moments slipped, drowned in
liquor and crushed under the
weight of promises broken.

But somewhere, in the quiet spaces
between, a small light began to
grow. I found fragments of laughter,
grains of peace, echoes of love
I thought had died.

In this light,
I could see myself. Not perfect,
but whole. Redemption isn't glory,
but a sunrise after endless nights.

I stand here now, forged in struggle,
holding joy with steady hands. This
is what it means to come back
to life.

THE CLEARING

For years, my path twisted.
Roots tangled with shadows,
branches heavy with false light.
With each step forward, I sank
deeper into questions dressed as
answers. Seeing faces wearing
borrowed truths.

The sky was always just out of
reach, painted with promises
that chipped away in the quiet
hours alone.

But one day, without thunder
or warning, the weight lightened.
Not because the world changed —
but because my need to understand
it fell away.

The fog didn't lift. I simply
stopped calling it "fog."
And there, in the same crooked
world where lies had once bloomed
like wildflowers, I stood still.
Not lost. Not found.
Just awake.

ACKNOWLEDGMENTS

First and foremost, I thank my creator who continues to guide me through the darkness into the light. Without that silent presence in my life, this book would have never been born.

Thank you to my family—Cameron, Mom, Dad, and Sis—for loving me even when I no longer loved myself. To those who stood by me when my world fell apart—BR and SP—your loyalty is etched in every page.

And to the broken and the healing, this book is for you.

ABOUT THE AUTHOR

Corey Weylon Gibson has been writing poetry since he was in grade school, but only recently found the courage to share it with the world. His poems are drawn from real experiences—decades spent navigating addiction, schizophrenia, heartbreak, recovery, and moments of unexpected grace. Writing became a form of survival for him, a way to make sense of the chaos and find meaning in the pain.

This collection is a reflection of his journey. His emotions are unfiltered, vulnerable, and surrounded by truth. No matter the content, Corey's desire is to connect with others who have struggled and remind them they're not alone.

When he's not writing, Corey works as an electrician and continues to pursue growth through meditation, mindfulness, and self-inquiry. He believes healing is possible and that poetry, in its purest form, can open the door to something greater. This is his first published work.

www.ingramcontent.com/pod-product-compliance
Lightning Source LLC
LaVergne TN
LVHW051431080426
835508LV00022B/3343